cover these pages with a collage of memories from your

First published by Jennifer Tookoian in 2014

Jennifer Tookoian
2037 W. Bullard #165
Fresno, CA 93711

www.itsallgoodbooks.com

978-0-9916461-4-2

Crayons, colored pencils and double stick tape work great for this book!

vacation. Use pictures, postcards or anything you like.

Color this! ↱

MY ORLANDO VACATION

NAME _____

DATE _____

Created by Jennie Tookoian
Designed & Illustrated by Elisabeth Markus

How this Memory Book Works

This is your book of memories. Be creative and make it your own. Don't worry about going in order - hop around from page to page. If you don't like a topic on the page, cross it out and change it, glue pictures over it or even tear it out and throw it away.

You can sketch your ideas or use a digital camera to snap your photos and glue them to your memory book. Find interesting things like shells, postcards or other things from your trip and glue them too. Print your pictures at your hotel while you are on vacation, or when you get home.

What you will need: a camera (if you want), pencils, markers, glue sticks, maybe scissors and your imagination.

Take advantage of the local resources. This means grab brochures, find postcards, things from the beach or in the hotel. Talk to the people who work there or live in Orlando. Cut out things you like and glue them into your book.

Make friends with the people around you. Have fun and make some memories.

We promise you, if you have fun with this and record your memories, you will have a great time reading it in 1, 5, or even 10 or more years from now. Enjoy!

This vacation **Memory Book** was created by

_____

What's the date of your trip?

How old are you?

Which cities are you traveling to or through?

Why are you going there?

Take a picture or sketch yourself from the beginning of your vacation... glue it here

Locate your trip on a **Global Map**. Draw a line from your home to your vacation spot. **Color** the map, use **stickers** or a *SYMBOL* like a ☆ to show your home and your vacation spot.

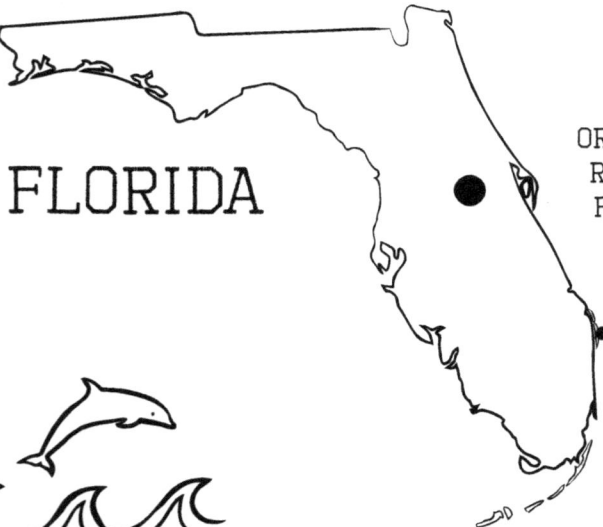

FLORIDA

ORLANDO DISNEY
RESORT AT THE
FOUR SEASONS

My first hour in Orlando...

The weather is:

It feels like:

I hear:

I smell:

I see :

The first thing I want to do is ...

The first thing I see in Orlando that I don't have at home is...

Take a photo or draw a **picture** of the view
from your hotel/bedroom window
(OR FIND A COOL PLACE IF YOU'VE GOT A CRUDDY VIEW... HEY, IT HAPPENS!)

Collect 6 things from the **resort**, the **park** or nature that are smaller than your palm. Photograph and/or glue them to this page. MAKE SURE NOT TO TAKE ANYTHING FROM PROTECTED AREAS SUCH AS STATE PARKS OR TIDAL POOLS.

1

2

3

4

5

6

Find a good place to watch the sunset. Take a **photograph** or SKETCH the sunset for a few days. Sketch or paste them here. *JOT DOWN THE DIFFERENCES BETWEEN THE DAYS.*

DAY 1

DAY 2

#1

#2

#3

The best one was...

LET'S EAT!!

1st Meal

where?   when?

rate it!

last Meal

where?   when?

Best Meal

where?   when?

Scavenger Hunt

RACE AGAINST A FRIEND TO FIND ALL OF THESE ITEMS, OR SET A GOAL FOR HOW LONG IT WILL TAKE YOU AND RACE AGAINST THE CLOCK TO BEAT YOUR TIME.

- [ ] someone crossing the street and looking at their cell phone
- [ ] an interesting person at the pool — create a story about them (you can use pages in the back)
- [ ] a baby sleeping
- [ ] someone with a sunburn
- [ ] Someone dancing
- [ ] two people wearing the same shirt
- [ ] a leaf that looks like an animal
- [ ] a family wearing mouse ears
- [ ] someone speaking another language
- [ ] someone humming or singing too loudly
- [ ] someone drinking a drink that has something in it (umbrella, flower, pineapple)
- [ ] an animal bigger than your hand
- [ ] a big boat
- [ ] someone with a moustache
- [ ] find out one reason Walt Disney chose Orlando for Disney World
- [ ] a set of twins
- [ ] find an annoying person and make them smile
- [ ] a waterfall
- [ ] a bratty kid
- [ ] someone with a flower in their hair
- [ ] an alligator (it doesn't have to be real)
- [ ] a screaming kid
- [ ] a plant that is taller than you
- [ ] eat a fruit grown in Florida
- [ ] someone wearing a ridiculous hat
- [ ] someone in a uniform
- [ ] a family playing on the "island"
- [ ] find out where the Everglades are located (...and, no, you can't just say Florida!)
- [ ] find out the name of at least one Native American tribe from Florida.

Can you find another kid working on this book too?

11

Apply glue here. Your items can be thick, thin, big, small, weird, interesting, funny, recycled, natural, unnatural, beautiful, ugly, bumpy, smooth, dead, living (no! just kidding!!! please, please, please don't do that!) Use just about anything that you think is awesome.

GLUE A BORDER ON THIS PAGE WITH
INTERESTING THINGS FROM YOUR TRIP
{ROCKS, LEAVES, WRAPPERS, LINT — ?!?}
GLUE A PICTURE OR A BUNCH OF PICTURES OF YOU
ON YOUR TRIP INSIDE THE BORDER.

WiLdLife Bingo

Try to fill up one row (across, down or diagonal). You can do this in a race against someone else or set a goal for how long it will take you and race against the clock. It might look a little funny, but feel free to yell "BINGO" when you complete it. (Listen for other kids yelling BINGO too!)

WHEN YOU FIND ALL THE THINGS IN A BOX, PUT A BIG X ON THAT BOX.

1 Lizard	2 alligators	4 colorful birds	A bunch of fish
6 butterflies	1 manatee	1 big fish	1 dragonfly
1 big dog with long black ears	1 duck	1 mouse with bow	1 mouse wearing gloves
3 palm trees	2 creepy insects	2 flamingos	1 snake

Strange Things...

Find and photograph or sketch different, interesting or strange things you have found in Orlando (people, insects, plants, waterfalls, etc).

Cut your photos in funky shapes to fit!

14

Tasty

Taste **4** new foods. What did you try? Where?
Photograph or sketch yourself eating one or more of the foods.

FOOD	WHERE I TRIED IT	DID I LIKE IT? Yes	No
1st _____		⟲	⟲
2nd _____		⟲	⟲
3rd _____		⟲	⟲
4th _____		⟲	⟲

Here is a picture of me trying a new food!

A BUGS EYE VIEW...

Lie on your back on the ground and look UP.

TAKE A PICTURE OR SKETCH WHAT YOU SEE FROM THIS DIFFERENT PERSPECTIVE.

Describe what you see in a couple of words.

...And a View from Above

Stand on the TALLEST place you can find
(TOP FLOOR OF YOUR HOTEL, A BALCONY, MOUNTAIN TOP, ETC.
JUST MAKE SURE IT IS A SAFE PLACE!)
Take a picture or sketch from this perspective. Describe what you see.

"ORLANDO ROCKS"

Design a t-shirt and a bumper sticker with a slogan or saying about your time in Orlando.

Orlando is for Kids!

COME TO ORLANDO...
IT'S THE BEST!

I ♥

Florida is great...see for yourself!

Nightlife!

What is the most memorable part about the night time in Orlando? What did you do or see at night? Take a picture or cut and glue pictures from brochures and postcards.

Describe what you see, hear, feel and smell.

Spot It

Record the BIGGEST or most interesting bugs you have seen in Orlando. Compare them to something else to describe the size.

The cockroach was bigger than my thumb!

THAT BUTTERFLY COULD HAVE EATEN A SANDWICH!

Wow that is OLD!

What is the oldest thing you have seen in Orlando?
Draw it or glue a picture. Describe it in one sentence.

PEOPLE ARE CRAZY!

What is the funniest or weirdest thing you have seen an adult do?
Describe it.

My FAVORITE Person
IN ORLANDO

Take a picture or make a sketch of your favorite person at your hotel/restaurant/activity center.

Glue it here.

THIS IS _____

WE MET AT _____

I LIKED HIM/HER BECAUSE _____

_____

23

SIGN *Language*

Can you find a sign in another language? Record the words.
Take a picture or sketch it. What does the sign mean? Translate it.
(HINT: ASK SOMEONE AT YOUR HOTEL, RESTAURANT, ETC.)

Hello
(English)

Hola
(Spanish)

Kon-nichiwa
(Japanese)

Halo
(Indonesian)

Sawubona
(Zulu)

Hei
(Finish)

Aloha
(Hawaiian)

Dzien'dobry
(Polish)

Sholem
Aley Chem
(Yiddish)

Bonjour
(French)

Guten Tag
(German)

Ni hao
(Chinese Manderin)

GUESS WHO☺?

When you are at the parks, at the pool, on an airplane or at your hotel, find the back of someone's head. Without looking at their face, guess what it looks like. Draw or describe their face below and check if you're right.

This is for the Birds!

Take a picture (or sketch) a **colorful** bird.
Describe where you saw it and anything else you know about it.

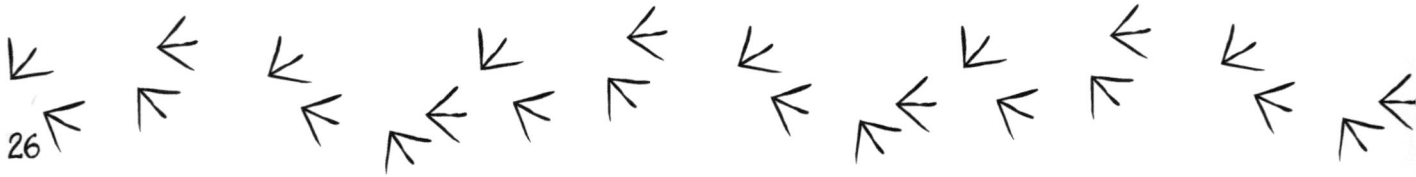

Nature Walk

Explore the nature in Orlando.
Take a picture or sketch the most interesting Plant or Flower.

OR YOU CAN GLUE A PETAL, LEAF OR BLOSSOM HERE.
DESCRIBE WHERE YOU FOUND IT AND ANYTHING ELSE YOU KNOW ABOUT IT.

ABC Vacation

Try to find something from your vacation — it can be anything — that starts with each letter of the alphabet!

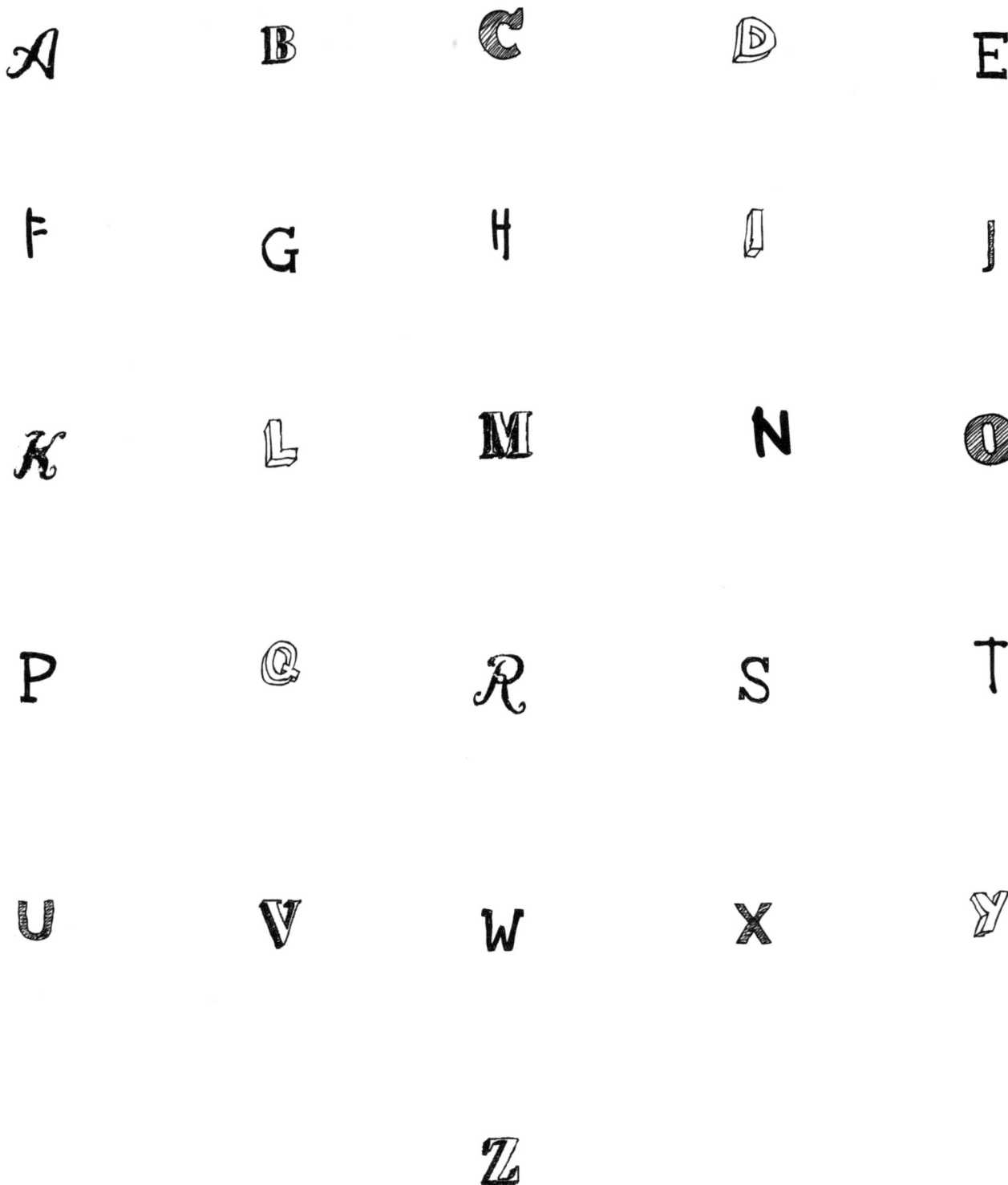

A   B   C   D   E

F   G   H   I   J

K   L   M   N   O

P   Q   R   S   T

U   V   W   X   Y

Z

Baaaaad memories!

("Uh, my mom forgot to pack my underwear." "The waiter dropped a plate of spaghetti on my head!" "We lived through a typhoon!")

What are some of the worst things that have happened on your trip?

Make list, take pictures, and/or glue something that reminds you of the worst things.

Weird things to do when you are bored...

Go to a crowded room/place of strangers and pretend you are a statue for 2 minutes. Count how many people notice you. Come up with 3 words or phrases to describe the experience. Take a picture of yourself or have someone take a picture of you while you are doing it.

Create your own Orlando drink. Come up with a tasty mix of flavors, juices, fruit etc. Write down the ingredients and give it a cool character name.

NAME OF DRINK

INGREDIENTS:

more weird things...

Find a famous or historical person that has been to Orlando or stayed in your hotel.
Hint: You can ask the people that work at the hotel, people in the town or read about the famous people in magazines or books about Orlando.

Dribble a few drops of pool water here. Glue some dirt and make a picture.

Collect straws, wrappers, paper coasters, mini umbrellas or other random things from the hotel or restaurants and glue them here...

another weird thing Vacation ORIGAMI

FIND THINGS TO MAKE.

Use a piece of scrap paper and fold it or shape it into something you have seen on your vacation like a waterfall, a palm tree... anything! Just get creative. If you really have a problem, you can wad up a piece of paper and call it a Florida orange! GLUE IT TO THIS PAGE.

Orlando Word Scramble

Can you make at least 15 words using the letters in ORLANDO, FLORIDA?
Answers in back...there are more than 100 words!!!

ORLANDO, FLORIDA

Answer Key on page 43.

My Last hour in Orlando

The weather is:_____

It feels like: _____

I hear _____

I smell _____

I see _____

The thing I will miss the most about Orlando is...

The first thing I want to do when I get home is ...

The best part of Orlando was...

GOOD TIMES

Glue Pictures or Postcards from your favorite things or places on your trip.

GOOD TIMES

Glue Pictures or Postcards from your favorite things or Places on your trip.

GOOD TIMES

Glue Pictures or Postcards from your favorite things or places on your trip.

GOOD TIMES

Glue Pictures or Postcards from your favorite things or Places on your trip.

GOOD TIMES

Glue Pictures or Postcards from your favorite things or places on your trip.

GOOD TIMES

Glue Pictures or Postcards from your favorite things or places on your trip.

GOOD TIMES

Glue pictures or postcards from your favorite things or places on your trip.

GOOD TIMES

Glue Pictures or Postcards from your favorite things or places on your trip.

Sample Pages

This is ... Jules ♥
WE MET AT the beach. she is [...]
I LIKED [...] BECAUSE [...]
and likes to swim [...]

Jules
Snorkel

This is for the Birds!
*Take a picture (or sketch) a **tropical** bird.*
Describe where you saw it, and anything else you know about it.

A bird from our hotel. It was in a big cage by the pool. It was noisy ♥!

Strange Things...
Find and photograph or sketch different, interesting or strange things you have found on this trip (people, insects, plants, waterfalls, etc.)
Awesome tree roots!
My Coconut Drink
A cool sand sculpture on the beach

ABOUT THE AUTHOR
Jennie Tookoian is a teacher who received her B.A. from UC Berkeley and her M.A. in Education from Stanford University. She now teaches in California's Central Valley and specializes in teaching writing to kids of all ages. The activities in this book are pulled from the prompts she uses in her writing classes. They have been road-tested by her students and her own three children.
You can find more information at www.itsallgoodbooks.com

ABOUT THE ILLUSTRATOR
Elisabeth Markus is a graphic designer and illustrator living in Central California with her husband and two children. Working as a freelance designer for 20 years through her graphic design studio Early Moon Design, she also has a positive t-shirt website, www.gladditudes.com.

Orlando Word Scramble (page 33) word list: DOORNAIL, LANDLORD, RAILROAD, RAINFALL, ANDROID, FORLORN, AFRAID, DOLLAR, FLORAL, INDOOR, INROAD, RADIAL, ADORN, ALOOF, DONOR, DRAIN, DRILL, DROID, DROLL, DROOL, FINAL, FLAIL, FLAIR, FLOOD, FLOOR, FRAIL, FRIAR, FROND, LOOFA, RADAR, RADIO, AFAR, ALAN, ARIA, ARID, DARN, DIAL, DILL, DINO, DODO, DOLL, DOOR, FAIL, FAIR, FALL, FIDO, FILL, FIND, FLAN, FOAL, FOIL, FOLD, FOND, FOOD, FOOL, FORD, IDOL, INFO, IRON, LAID, LAIN, LAIR, LAND, LARD, LIAR, LILO, LION, LOAD, LOAF, LOAN, LOON, LORD, NAIL, ODOR, ORAL, RAID, RAIL, RAIN, RAND, RIND, ROAD, ROAR, ROLL, ROOF, ADD, AID, AIL, AIR, ALL, AND, DAD, DID, FAD, FAN, FAR, FIN, FIR, FOR, ILL, ION, LAD, LID, NIL, NOD, OAF, OAR, ODD, OIL, OLD, RAN, RID, ROD, AN, DO, IF, IN, NO, OF, ON, OR

www.ingramcontent.com/pod-product-compliance
Lightning Source LLC
Chambersburg PA
CBHW050452110426
42744CB00013B/1974